# I Sing to the Greenhearts

# I Sing to the Greenhearts

*Maggie Harris*

Seren is the book imprint of
Poetry Wales Press Ltd.
Suite 6, 4 Derwen Road, Bridgend,
Wales, CF31 1LH

www.serenbooks.com
Follow us on social media @SerenBooks

The right of Maggie Harris to be identified as
the author of this work has been asserted in accordance
with the Copyright, Designs and Patents Act, 1988.

ISBN: 978-1-78172-771-3
ebook: 978-1-78172-773-7

A CIP record for this title is available from the British Library.

The publisher acknowledges the financial assistance of the Books Council of Wales.

Cover artwork: *House in Stanleytown* by James Mingo

Printed in Bembo by 4Edge ltd, Hockley.

# Contents

# I Sing to the Greenhearts

I sing to the greenhearts; don't you remember me?
The curly-haired girl from Main Street
warned not to wheel her bike on the backdam
where the road became track became bush became
the unnavigated wild for a girlchild.

How can you not know me when my heart dropped
down over the stelling to watch the waters
swirl about you in a feast of crabs and mud?
All I knew was *greenheart nevah rot so they tek he*
*all across the world for harbouration.*

No one let our forest sing, the whine
of chainsaws cut out their harmonies, only cries of fallen
sloth and capuchins screaming      birds rising
flame into a dust-bowl sky.

Keep to Main Street, they said. Do not go wandering
into the bush, there are only murderers there, and ghosts
mad men with cutlasses and quicklime
searching for the way home since slavery time.

The parrots now, so many mothers stoned
to the ground so their babies can inhabit the shoulders
of men and girls, my grandmother even, the soul
of kindness, mother of so many children I lose count.

There's Polly the parrot on the veranda
endlessly singing her name *prettypollyprettypollypretty.*

No-one let the forest sing      they were too busy stripping
her flesh and bones      crunching into dust
undiscovered potions and vaccines.      No-one sung to me
of forests, no one taught me to love them
no one brought me the tale of lilies as wide
as a boat                only
stories of running men and crazy
women mad with snakebite hollow with gold

and cloven footed Cinderellas
tip tap toe in the deep dark woods *Bye Baby Bunting*
*Daddy's gone a-hunting.*

So they're saying now there are not enough
trees to filter the carbon to allow us to
breathe. The politician and his cowboys tear through
verdant forests     like a virus     razing
them to the ground.          I potter round my garden like
it's the world. We're all migrants here, Japanese bananas, Chinese fuchsias,
Welsh poppies, me.

In my dreams, I sail with Captain Cook,
not Columbus, who never knew where
he was going even when he got there.
I am a plant collector, sleeping
in a cabin with the artists and scientists.
I try to organise a mutiny.

# The Daydream, *Dante Gabriel Rossetti*

You, Jane, are the first thing I see: you,
in your velveteen bed of sycamore forest,
your tresses of russet, the fallen rose
in your calamine palm, the open book.

Dream me beautiful to the cusp
of pain to splinter and woodlouse
to the last panther
to howler monkeys screaming
from the edges of the New World.

# I dream of balconies

fretwork balconies in Castries     balconies of wood and iron
intricate as lace     balconies bursting with ixora in Havana
blood red geraniums in Catalonia     purple petunias in Albufeira
morning glories blue as the Virgin in Santiago     passion flowers
wild and rampant in Tobago

there must be room for a rocking chair, a Juliet balcony will not do
there must be room for it to rock, rocking chairs roll as they rock
are percussion to the rhythm of your lullaby     cradle the cry
of the child at your breast     echo the womb lulling you to
a timeless sleep     *brownskin girl stay home and mind baby*

chair and floor must be made of wood
coarse or grained     knotted or polished to a sheen
only wood can carry the sound of love     only wood
can recognise the code of the woodpecker
only wood can inhabit the smell of rain
remember the clutching fingers of the iguana
the cautious slow she climbed

leave me here where the jasmine will enfold me, and time anoint me
not with the memory of massa's pale wife, her hands flailing as she waves
but Frida's gardenias, in the South American feast of my childhood.

# Goa

I belong in a garden like this          fairy lights strung tree to tree
candles flickering like nymphs          bats streaming overhead

we scan the menu in the half-light      waiters flit between the tables
and the bare shoulders of women         who have spent all day at the beach

I belong in a garden like this          the sea a whisper away
keeping the secrets of my kin           who sailed from Portuguese shores
to worship here in houses of dark wood      at altars with silver candlesticks

outside this ring of trees scooters whizz all day and night
streets throng with the children of de Gama, four strong
on pillion, stalls bow with gold and tin, leather and plastic
melon juices spill on the bare feet of the woman begging for rupees

but the bats are here          elemental     mythic
owning the blackness of caves where souls dwell      their accusatory fingers

of flight

# Tamarind

it's not that i miss tamarind balls mashed up in my palm
squashed by my thumb      licking it clot by sticky clot
on its way to my mouth         it's not that i miss the fiery sweetness
of it the sweet/sour taste rolling over on my tongue

is we get brought up not to be lawless
'lawness' mean *don't spread you legs too wide too quick*
*bare you bubby in public   wine yuh ass*
'wine' mean *flounce, undulate, roll your backside*

but watch your mouth mind your ps and qs
keep the brown low
accentuate your blue eyes and your 'good' hair

but i born already having the hot mouth of the devil child
whose sassiness delighted every rum-drinker
my daddy bring to the front porch who name themselves
coloured   dougla   malatta   and loved a blue eye child

i learn men love full lips
like the porn girls you see everywhere now
paying money to inject God knows what to plump up
and pump up just so you could      *well you know*

back there on our front steps
the visitors put on rubber slippers and sat down
pretending to like tamarind         you're welcome we said
you're welcome but Girl get Mister a plate

maybe if my father's red skin didn't have a Bajan
grandpappy somewhere back before certificates
interrupting the bloodline       mixing up the blood

ripping the connection between ebony and string
instruments somewhere in the region of Senegal
the dis-placement dis-membering
wouldn't be wide as the Caribbean Sea

and learning sometimes too late
that not all fruit travel well
some need the very air of a home-place
to grow sweet and fall in her own sweet time
slow-slow off the vine

and if i could go back there
on my front porch eating tamarind balls
or whatever in season
well lawd i would be as lawless as i could
and let my housedress drop between my knees
like a hammock catching every drop of juice
falling from my mouth and say
now tell me a *different* story

## My Banana thinks on Louise Bennett's 'Colonisation in Reverse'

Somewhere in his roots there must have been a séance,
these things can cause revolts. Rumour spreads.
Several times the wind was a banshee he thought
only existed in Jamaica (he had of course
never been to Jamaica – his birthplace was
a greenhouse someway south of Hemel Hempstead)
100 decibels over land and sea, souls screaming
in several octaves      which, on occasions, would bring rain.
Objects would fly his way – next door's washing,
a trampoline. The state of his leaves broke
him: like jhandi flags weather-frilled and ripped
in some sun-bleached front yard in Tobago
where the use of the word *hurricane* was not unusual.

When she came back from Spain, the woman who had patted
him into this soil stood at the back door and hollered
'O my God! My God! I planted one banana and I come back to three!'
For a moment he thought he was a refugee. He'd wondered then
if the Light and the Sword had touched him,
he heard such frequent references from those close by –
the ginger lily and the cocos capitata were always
in the throes of gossip, swapping tales of home soil
and temperatures in Biblical persuasions.
He considered these testaments anecdotal, his own settlement
had been without drama. His trunk and plumes
may well be towering above this backyard fence but
he had no control over any of it. If his roots
wanted to replicate and emerge with paddle shaped leaves
that became percussion when the winds came, well
that was up to them. He had no part in it,
happy just admiring the parakeets screeching
like fishwives in the chestnut trees, tall enough
to look over the gardens, spewing hot tubs. It was sky,

not earth, in which he dwelt. But somehow the earth
was sending him messages: voices of the dead tapping
into the watercourse, reaching up into his thirsty throat
singing *we shall overcome*. And sometimes,
just sometimes he could hear drums,
which strangely made him wish
he could just pick his feet up        and run.

# Clematis, early flowering

Miss Show-her-face has shown her face at last.
Two years now we've had the in-out out-in dance
in a pot, in the ground, in the shade, in the sun.
The pampering went on for a long time.
I baby her because that's what you do
with something delicate and young. You mother.

A flower came last year, just one. Whether
was rain or sun cause her to shrivel –
who knows? I had others to mind.
In May she shivered like a queen in her pot
outside the greenhouse door.
When her roots touched earth
was like tornado twist the yard
and strip just her of all her leaves.
It could have been the slugs.

Trying to prepare her for the world
my words were harsh: *Stop your snivelling
and just bloody grow*. She must have heard.
She must have come to in her own sweet time
to drop the attitude and just get on with life.
See her now clambering up the fence
her head a mass of blooms, blue as morning glory.
I'm just happy at last she's seen some sense.

# Sweet Pea

if you decide to ask these ladies in don't wait
for the stories of them raring to run out the door
g/r/ow
t
a
l
l
and fragrant
promiscuous as hell fearing nothing

it'll trip off your tongue     comparisons to the roaring twenties
dilettantes who could
 j i t t
        e r
            b u g and Charleston into Tuesday
for they need the loving, Mister, never mind they quickstep
into life polishing their faces before its time

they're fickle for fickle sake so
love them gentle and love them strong
corral their trembling legs with whatever the fuck slugs hate
have a rum and coke while you wait
or a gin        and prepare to catch them when they
fall         their broken heads dipping     like a bird

# My Fuchsia Likes Reggae

It's not that he don't like hiphop or jive
or rock and roll or Steve Wright's Love Songs
on a Sunday. He's been known

to chill at Gregory Porter, his love drops
hanging suggestively over the rim of his pot.
But Reggae is the thing, the other Gregory

(Isaacs) *Night Nurse*, Peter Tosh, Toots,
(God rest). It must be the roots thing
licking him right down to the compost

thirty minutes of that limping rhythm
injecting his leaves with luminosity
only usually seen after rain. His

love drops get flushed with the red
of cockscombs, flashed with the purple
of Lent, frilled with the effervescent spray

of longing. Mr Fuchs now, dedicated designator
of genera, died before his name was given
to this son of the tropics, by a brother from Hispaniola

*Father Charles Plumier*
for whom 'discovery' and naming paved the way
for passages across the seas and gardens

dedicated to hybridity.
All that may be history as they say
what's the point in the remembering?

But here's the thing – memory
still living through rhythm
through cells and cymbals    through drumbeats

through pistils and sepals
water, blood and soil
like gangsters in a shoot-out.

In this English garden Reggae's king
and Fuchsia reigns.

# Mister Arum

Mister Arum
in his white sombrero.
Mr Cool in the heat breaking
out against this seaside earth so
dark and rich you'd never know
just down the road the chalk cliffs
loom white as history. Two summers
now he's sulked, longing for Wales, its damp
earth, the company of ferns.
*Do something for chrissake*, I said. *Grow.*

Now slow as a Mexican wave he's adding
his white suit to the display
in this anarchic garden with its red rhodies
and yellow poppies and deep
magenta geraniums. Maybe
he was just waiting to bring
something beautiful to the table.
Some of us just take a little more time.

# The Tree Fern Remembers

listening to Massive Attack at Eden
that summer of dreams – pre-COVID – when crowds came
to imagine themselves in forests of rain and deserts of agave

their rhythms vibrated through the tunnels of earth
                the china clay pits of St Austell
reverberating through pyramids of glass, the Biome

the beautiful gathered at the Baobab Rum Bar
danced on the lawns   their palms
like visors against the sun

we were beautiful and free    carried Eden home
in the shape of a tree    planted him amongst friends,
canna lilies    cabbage palms        cordylines

now when it rains we stand underneath his leaves
talking story of Tasmania and leylines under the sea
where the riddum will find us wherever we be
back home children still thirsty for our ancestry

# Mr Plantain

Mr Plantain tek a long time to mek up his mind
if he green or yellow
Mr Plantain don't know if he want to be fufu
or plantain chips
he don't know if he gon be slice long and fry
and sit pon the side of chicken and rice
Mr Plantain travel from Brixton to Broadstairs
on special order for one woman who know his name
who neva mistake he for no junior half ass banana
sprawlin all ova the damn place

Mr Plantain tek he revenge from all dem
who drag he from the plantation
bring he to a cold country to mash, chip or slice
sprinkle with salt and fry in oil
so he tek he own time to turn yellow from green
from hard to soft
in somebody half-light kitchen
where he stretch he long boomerang
indolent
lazy
delicious
self
like a tomcat
inch by every
glorious
plantain
inch.

# A Pandemonium of Parrots

My kitchen window is a portal: conversations stutter
between the parakeets and the radio
callers on the line pouring their sadness
into the ears of Jeremy Vine and a million
listeners stirring a cup of tea.

It hurts to listen to the stories coming
from deep in the throat, farewells denied, bedside
goodbyes uttered over the phone.
'We told him that we loved him', the caller's
voice cracked on the line, 'the girls too.
They're just old enough to understand
he won't be coming home.'

The birds are even louder now the streets
no longer scream. It's spring and the air
is filled with jays, woodpigeons, herring-gulls,
crows. Parakeets shoot like arrows from the trees.
'I'm sorry for your loss, I'm sorry for your loss.'
Stories come more frequently, another broken soul:
this one was just a boy, just a boy.

My telephone brings my mother's voice,
She's 85, alone. Her scattered memories of other times,
another country, itself in lockdown now. Unimaginable

all that sun, where parakeets and parrots bright as zinnias
anoint the sky. Her scattered memories spark
my isolated air: we are in a bubble she and I.
I tell her about the parakeets. 'Chin up,' she says,
'Chin up. This too will pass. This too will pass.'

# Her Wedding Dress

Swinging from the washing line
taffeta and lace, faded now and limp
it lilts into the screech of herring gulls
and the dives of crows      from a grey
un-anointed sky devoid of hummingbirds

67 years in the dreamtime
the dress like a child's    a doll child
a child so small she had no breasts
a bra had to be sculpted out
of feathers                     bust

-darts like invisible arrows
shooting from waist to chest

the story leaked out over time
she never suckled her own mother's breasts
gone too soon to the grave with ague

the sweetheart neckline promised
a bittersweet notion of bliss
a child in a lace wedding dress
could just so become Mistress

stitched into the seams
tiny running stitches
buckled hand-sewn zip
another woman's story bleeds
from brown-skinned hands
moving from plantation lands
through the eye of the needle and the sewing machine
to become a woman of means
a Caribbean Arachne

hand-sewn stitches tight and small
taffeta so aged gone soft
she can hardly imagine herself that bride
in taffeta stiff from the store

it has no business here
and maybe i
should have let it rest
in its bundled bed
instead of bringing it out into this air
as if it had another chance of life.

# Head of a Mulatto Woman

*After Jackie Kay, 'Fanny Eaton, the Pre-Raphaelite Jamaican Muse'*

I see you, Fanny, in the heat of Jamaica:
Bathsheba's fingers weaving your hair into plaits
your head wedged between her knees
just like my mother, my sister, on the porch.

I see you, Fanny, in Wiltshire, where my cousin's
beauty equals yours, her hair natural, unfettered
raising a house of Caribbean children
on an English council estate

I see you, Fanny, in all the aunts that still surface
from Ohio to the Nederlands, brownskin women
whose internal worlds shift nightly
from the Indies to (still) surprise in cities

Jackie looks for you in corridors
seeking lineage in black grandmothers
adorning the white walls
peopled from the colonial halls of plenty

And everything they don't know I can tell you
but first let me borrow your pearls
that lustre, like small moons
on the canvas of your skin.

# Only these grandmothers

Only these grandmothers can see down the long road travelled
where all the love and pain converge like cars in a traffic jam.
Only these grandmothers carry the scent of kitchens
infused with wild garlic to layer
the earthenware pots where rabbits simmer.

Only these grandmothers smell of milks suckled at the breasts
of Amazons and lowly country women whose babies
make do with Cow & Gate, make room
for others who will inherit the world.

There are grandmothers who left those kitchens long ago
for factories and offices, where the typing pool
and the cleaning women all walk on rollercoaster ledges,
keeping their determined stares ahead, not looking
back the way they came where sheer edges
mark the abyss of failing
to be mother/ father/ provider/ teacher.

Generations on, the mother's sleep is haunted by dreams
of a succubus inhabiting her body and soul. When every fever
of your child ushers in the terror of gravestones
fists beating where the heart should be
pounding into midnight     the long hours cloaking
the bedroom floor with a terror     unnamed.

Blessed are those who remember the burial place
of the navel string.
Blessed are those whose faces still glow faintly in daguerreotypes
whose gold bangles circa 1903 swing from the wrists of a favourite child.
Blessed are those whose memories string like fairy lights
between balconies and high-rise flats          villages of lamplight
country lanes and cane fields          blackberry bushes and mango trees.

Only these grandmothers can raise their rifles over the gates and shoot
into the trees where the limbs of young men     flail into the foliage.
Only these grandmothers can halt the slingshots aimed at birds
in the knitted palms of their hands. Only these grandmothers can look
down the long roads travelled and back to the future
where the children test the waters with their toes
and languages ricochet like gunshots.

# Honeysuckle in the Hedgerows

I      am my mother's eyes
I brave the Cornish coast path
its' jagged death-wish cliffs
chevronned quartz and granite
daring me to look down at sea
hammering its anger on rocks
as black as Pembrokeshire.

I      am my mother's feet
place them one before the other
testing the unholy ground, deep scars
gouged by rain and I can't imagine
her here in her size three sandals;
*Margaret!* she would say,
*What are you doing here girl? You will fall!*

I      am walking for her because she never will
I am seeing for her because she never will
now she can only shuffle short distances
around her Council bungalow, or Tesco
on a Friday accompanied by a daughter.

I      am listening for my mother.
I am listening
as she struggles to hear on the telephone
and will not hear these grasshoppers
zinging through the gorse
or witness butterflies
in the scabious.

I      walk outside the borders as I always have
wanting to be the seer of a thousand things
I've never seen
follow a perilous path I've never been
so I can say, there is honeysuckle in the hedgerows
and its scent hangs on the Cornish air
anoints you like incense, flushed with the salt of the sea
and, look, this is what I saw
here, is where I've been.

# Although i come from a Land of Many Waters

Although i come from a land of waters
i did not swim them
Although i come from a land of mountains
i did not climb them
Although i come from a land of savannas
where vaqueros roost
their cattle and Roraima rises
above the clouds
i did not know them

      but when we drove into Cumberland
and the roads emptied of traffic     silent wheels
rolling       through quiet pastures
and walls of stone      each bend
opened to a new promise     a ribbon of light
flashed into paintings by Monet and Seurat
i saw them      my first fells rising
in shifting contours    light and shade

i wanted to leave the car and run
feet bare through fields of fern and sheep
like puffs of abandoned cloud   and throw myself
into the lake      its waters clear as glass creating fictions
at the water's edge where fells submerged
into another world      a world half known
and longed for   of watercourse

and caves, canyon and chasm
forged by riverine tongues on their journey from Roraima

my mouth was full of words but no words fell
they swum, contained, like the child i carried
swimming in her world of dawn    secured
by the mountain of my body

# Paper Patterns

The face of the government official on page 2 is no longer recognisable:
his right ear is missing and his cheekbone snipped to a perfect curve
where the collar will rest, a 'sweetheart' collar, she says and shows me
the magazine where Julie Andrews is in lemon cotton, edged with lace.
She particularly likes the frock Gina Lollobrigida is wearing, but Daddy
won't like that, she says, it will look out of place.

She won't cut the pages of the magazines that bring slices of lives
of which she could only dream, but *The Chronicle* is fine, it's only the price
of sugar and riots again last week. It's the perfect paper, long
enough for bodices, sashes, trousers even but she's not ready for those,
not quite yet, she doesn't know a single soul who wears *those*
apart from the doctor's wife who hasn't realised she's no longer in America.

The scissors have a coarser sound when travelling along the floor
a louder, more determined score along the line of chalk, smooth
decisive clips, knowing they have a goal to reach, splitting his cheek
and the photo of the Nestle baby, fast asleep.
There's a wholesome hum when paper is pinned to cotton, train
– tracked by a line of pins plucked from in-between her teeth

the scissors buoyed with the impossible weight of dreams.
She needs my hand to hold all still, even the lightest breeze
through the jalousies can lift and tease, causing the wrong cut,
the wrong rip. Fragments only fit for paper dolls I'll make –
whose fragile, un-gendered selves will remain conjoined.

## Elegy for the dysfunctional and
## remind me again who

So now i'm talking to the dads one by one and i have to keep things nice
there's no room for anger here, anger has swept by – black and thunderous

palpitating like a heart that has lost its rhythm, so many voices
vibrating outwards from rolling walls of text messages

words indelible – my skin is alive with them,
they have tattooed themselves in frantic disorder

*you wouldn't **believe** what she's **done** now thrashed the **house***
*threw a **stone** through the **window i had** to call the police out again*

*oh my **god that's** so not the **truth he** had me by the **hair***
*kicked me **in the belly** i swear on **my baby's** life that's the **truth***

i can feel my father rolling over and over in his grave never thought
i'd say i'm glad he's dead    he would wish he was dead the shame

the babies are edible and lovely, they grow in teenage bellies like grapes
attached to the vine *who's the daddy* suddenly there are strangers in your life

and Facebook private lives spattered across TikTok mantras to 3000 followers
*and I said to him I said **no-one's going** to fuck with me anymore*

all the while the babies are huggable lovable little squashy things in snowsuits
easy to play pass the parcel overnighting with daddyo or auntieo or Tommy

from upstairs *who's harmless really.* And who will notice she needs changing
when everyone's skinning up downstairs. Don't think. Don't think. Don't.

You've been here before. Remember. 13 she was then 13. Off to kick
the world. Fuck ballet.

**Don't** because when you bring her home you can't pretend she's yours
you can't pretend to tuck her beneath your mummy wings your granny
        wings

for someone will come for her just when she's settled in the new school
at ballet or Beavers or panto or parties with friends who have daddies

*you want to come with Mummy now dontcha doncha*
and the social wring their hands in the shadows *let's see let's see let's*

and your heart will be broken like biscuits they throw on the carpet
while screaming *i want my mummy i want my mummy iwant*

# Testimony to a cradled phone not in your pocket

*In the beginning there were telephones    fat black ones like beetles    we never had*
*one    my father used a conch        still does most nights from somewhere off the coast*
*of Barbados*

all night long I think of calling you, the thought   keeps me awake
I wrestle the sheets    and pillows with such vigour we're in a battle zone
Sun-up takes its time      night-time stretched so far   so wide   one minute
I'm on Easter Island the next I'm on  Goree              Nureyev was there
and Carlos Acosta   they never looked at me   just kept on dancing    even
though my mouth was a fish  falling out of the sea

                                                            Havana
turned up in an advert for perfume      a ship's figurehead   a woman's
silicone breasts          just like the one I watched from the narrow street
negotiating a passage    through the black balconies of hotels
leaning close as        conspirators

I can't count the cost in years or classrooms you refused to enter   your legs
kicking the welfare    worker      I can't count the ballet fees
or certificates   or the tattoos        like bruises or your      disfigured feet

I should have called you Ariel      I should have known   instead
I went for fairy tales and warned you        please save your tears Alice
for a real crisis       the years are dominoes falling        1987, 93,
the Millennium    video montages    you age 3        looking back at me
from the arms of your father       practising pirouettes on a stage
of bears and gnomes        knocking    your head against the wall
words falling from your fist

you aged 13 on the doorstep demanding y/our stereo   the car waiting
your *fuck-yous* amplified        in our quiet seaside street.
*Where was the child   the soft-down black-haired beauty scissored out of my womb*
*who set the stage alight?*

I longed to know your wild but my body did not want to remember wildness
slept beneath my skin   our people thrust out into the *wilderness*     500 years
of nights and days  bearing scourges tunnel-deep    from Goree
to the Southern shores bound rib to thigh   the same ocean
they laid those cables       their ships bucking the winds
from County Kerry to America

the years are dominoes falling        telephones in their cradles waiting
until the cradles      ceased to be   in their place   all the music in the world
drawn from the breath      of flutes and bugles   talking drums    choirs
and testaments      jingles    synthesisers     and a million parents rejoicing
at last! there *will* be a voice there *will* be a voice   there *will* be a voice
at the end of the invisible line   and always
you could        *leaveamessageleaveamessageleavealeavealeaveleave*

*in the beginning there were telephones   fat black ones like beetles   we never had one*
*my father used a conch   still does   from somewhere off the coast of Barbados*
*i call him sometimes   sometimes he answers*

# The Coloured Girl Speaks of the Colour of Words

*Emancipate yourself from mental slavery*
*None but ourselves can free our mind*
– Bob Marley, "Redemption Song"

I
Could say that I was not black enough
or white enough
or woman enough
or man enough
or mother enough
or father enough
or innocent enough
or enlightened enough
or political enough
or culturally active enough
or pinned to the body-mast enough
or whalebone to the sea enough
in the microplastic tsunami of my generation

I
could say that I was not lyrical enough
or raw spitting spoken-word enough
I could wash my hands right now
– Lady Macbeth of the West Indies –
of the small murders and intimacies
on the way to becoming
someone's native
someone's definition of
any drop of existentialist blood
that made me what I am

I
could blame any lover for the lack of me
anyone who sees my colour before they see me
anyone in the tick-box of power
who placed me in the category *Other*
those in the plantation chair rocking on white balconies
would have me remain in the shadows of the greenheart tree
so I would never be white enough
or black enough

or acid-tongued enough
or representative enough
to package or market
to transfer the guilt of generations
that lurk beneath each ejaculation.

But
the suitcase I carried from
the New World to the Old
was made of alligator skin
seamed with the unwritten tears and strangled voices
of those whose colour was all washed out
stained to an indeterminate brown of rivers and semen
so muddy, their language became the scream of capuchins
the burning ash of cane
the muzzle of the manatee
the roots of the banana tree where
Aloyius Benedictine lies buried
the noose still around his neck.

But
our language is also
the vibration of home-made guitars
the self-taught melody of mouth organs
the ornate passage of tabernacles
the ink-stained hallelujahs whose
proclamations of promise
rise high in the Amens of the faithful
high in the signatures of egrets across
a Demerara evening sky
high in the creativity of those who dare to inscribe
their dreams like oil on water in the mouth of the Orinoco
high with the words of Marley
*Emancipate yourself from mental slavery*
*None but ourselves can free our minds ...*
So          this is a Praise Song for the enough of us
we are enough in the transcribing of us
we are enough
we are enough
I        am enough.

# Uploading the zeitgeber

mi-phone loves that i hold him closer than a lover
mi-phone loves that he is the dawn now
a Eucharist glowing in the still-dark mornings
come to light with mi scrolling

mi-phone cares not that he fractures my sleep
he knows he is mi raison d'être
loved up with the relentless patrolling of his body
sleek and promiscuous as vertigo

mi-phone's surreptitious stalking stylishly
transforms each moment into memes
fingers become the tool with which to connect
with the world,  thumbs
endlessly scrolling from *like* to like

mi-phone make it so we no longer need words
in-built responses say it so much better
gifs & hearts, double hearts, triples
*thank you  thank you so much that's beautiful  so cool!*
*Congratulations!!! WoW! Happy birthday!*

Sunday mornings mi fingers no longer remember what they used to do
tiptoe under the sheets down the length of mi lover's body where his pen
is lies waiting to be awoken   rise   to a mourning of love

mi-phone has appropriated these fingers since dawn
mi eyes can scan the world
a torrent in Kathmandu, olive trees torched in Palestine
more lives upturned in the Channel

mi-phone knows we can't go back to the dream
that our bodies once knew when to succumb
to the almost death of the dark  where men lay down their swords
and slept                 instead, these days, silver surfers ride
black holes believing them to be
the sisters of stars            startlingly, increasingly, distant

# Black on White and Falling

*(Oradour-sur-Glane)*

Their faces burn in my memory
like posters of the missing
black and white squares on a white wall
no, not missing. Dead.
Cauterized. Extinguished.

black and white on a white wall

.... .... .... .... .... ....           white spaces bleed like negatives
....                                   those for whom there are no photographs
                                          their names like scribbles in the sand

.... .... .... .... .... ....

photographs
reserved for newsreels
and formal moments – baptisms, weddings,
funerals

schoolchildren grouped in the playground
their faces staring out through time
Marie, Michelle, Gilberte ...
                    grizzled old men in Sunday Best
                           young women, hair upswept, their rounded
                           cheeks, a smile unfolding
                           a mother, a daughter, her arms draped over
                           her sister
infants, their small faces
like suns in the white froth of lace, their christenings
performed in the font in the very church
where on 10th June 1944 the town would be herded
like sheep, the doors barred, grenades tossed

Now, photographers
scramble over broken walls
peer through windowless fragments of rooms
pose their children at gravestones
aim their mobile phones
at Singer machines and iron bed frames
twisted and mangled from the flames

when we leave, like moles
to stagger back into the world
we notice the others we had missed
in the exhibition space:
Africans; Hutus, Tutsis
in sharpened digital images
just like the ones we're used to
spiralling like atoms
through our TV screens, Facebook, and instagram
Hanoi
Cologne
Beirut
Kabul
Mosul
Baghdad
Gaza
... ...  ...  ... ... ... ...  ... ... ...
... ...  ...  ... ...
...

# OIL and WATER

*Guyana Guyana Land of Many Waters*
*Guyana Guyana Land of Many Waters*

there are refugees now in
the Caribbean Sea     fleeing from
starvation     no electricity
Venezuelans crossing the Gulf of Paria
small boats rocking in the rough
black waters     listen to their cries in the wind.

***Oil and Water don mix let me tell you***
***Oil and Water don mix***

in Trinidad oil made some rich
now oil and gas both pumping
and the rich stay rich but the poor stay poorer
what will happen in Guyana?

***Oil and Water don't mix lemme tell you***
***Oil and Water don't mix***

who remember the man with the ink stain hands
draw round the shape of a calabash bowl
drip his quill in the ink with his long white hands     said
*here* this land is *Mine*
*Mine Mine*

***Who give him permission?***
no parrot no jaguar no labba
***Who give him permission?***
no agouti no camoodi no man
atee
***Who give him permission?***
no greenheart no mora no crabwood no ants no cassava

*Mine Mine Mine*

Raindrop pause in the centre
of falling say *yes absolutely*
place this teardrop on the Spaniard side          this one on the Dutch side
this one on the English side
*yes absolutely*

The river running crazy like a wild man          from way up *who know where*
some mountain top some stream    he and Mister Rain in liaison   spit
and bubble and run   he get the conversation going    get the conversation
flowing       river turn waterfall   waterfall to rapid    fullflow   jungle flow
catapulting downwards singing all kind of chorus *down to the river/down to the
river*   cutting through the jungle    hollering and warning **get out the way!**
swallowing whole trees and mangrove roots  tumbling alongside piranha
and water-snake   eel and otter   all living and eating and mating and dying
riverbed trembling with bones with fossils calcium deposit     and the gold
the gold the sought-for gold    mercury and   belly-up fish   so   if he have a
chance to swallow and drown and chop and slice is do he do

*what he know about responsibility*
*responsibility*
*responsibility?*
*does he know that the trees are our lungs?*
*just over the border now the men with machetes*
*slice and burn chop and burn and who know the names of the silent people*
*hiding in the wake of the chop down trees*
*did anyone **ask them? anyone ask them?***
*did anyone know their names? did anyone say **is this your land your land?***

speaking for the water remember Mama Wata remember the daughters
stolen from Africa searching for the Goddess who couldn't remember
          her name
speaking for the water     *O Land of Many Waters Guyana Guyana*

But now the black gold find is a different thing is a different thing altogether
is na jus cutlass, is na just woodcutter, na just driller an digger wukkin hand
in han na jus a coolie man nar a black man not Wai Wai not Macusi    for oil
and water no mix mek i tell you oil and water don mix

**Oil and water don mix   mek i tell you**
**Oil and water don mix**

41

and who will take us to Omai?
now that Wilson Harris has gone
who will take us to Omai? who
will row us across guide us across the

**deep**

          **black**

                               **satin**
                             **black**

**w  i  l  d  e  r     n    e    s    s**
all the red and white of us   all the yellow and black of us
all the plantation children of us
all the overseer massa pickney   all the blu eye long hair of us
all the dougla the curlyhair
the poets all   the rabbis  the obeahmen  the pundit  all

*for Oil and Water don mix don mix*
*Oil and Water don mix*
*Oil and Water don mix*

# Lilith

You shouldn't have died like that. Hounded like a thief through remorse-less Borth, hiding under caravans instead of roaming forests and steppes, your eyes golden in the dark. What did you dream of? There beneath the caravan, the carapace, pseudo tin-can home, housing the dreams of those seeking solace. Seeking nature? Nature came to *them*, and they didn't know it: a lone young lynx tasting freedom, salt air in your nostrils, acrid log fires, the dank impervious fear of humans.

Beauty can be a curse. You were used to being stared at, through bars and filtered lenses. They professed to love you but didn't know how. Did you sense the death of your kin? Strangled by a noose in clumsy hands? Did you hear their hearts race then slow? If they had lived, what communion would there have been? Would you have told them of the earth beneath your feet, the wind in the hills, the rushing song of streams? Would they have said, *Run for me Lilith, as I cannot?*

Lilith, Lilith! Who named you for the Goddess they called a demon? Who spread the lie that your feline life as female was something to be feared? Was it fear of you that drove them to hunt you down? Or fear of the pack behind them, each one charging the other with their own twisted truths? Did your heart race then slow in the blast from a stalking gunman? Run free now, Lilith. Enter the wild they denied you. Run.

# The Migration of Ghosts

In the country where I was born they said the dead couldn't swim
and migration frees you from their ghosts, their constant whimpering
on what you should or shouldn't have done. There in the land
of massacre there's still a scramble to leave, body or no body and some
of them hitch rides on mobile phones or tankers while some try floating
as they heard it might help with questions of identification.
I saw them myself in the Azores, their bones granulated
to form coral and even undersea they gleam with what
one might describe as a wavering hue. But I was young then
and fanciful, and not everything I say is true.

Here in my final years I could live nowhere but the sea. I tried
the country once and all it did was eat me. So I've managed
to build a body without bones and these sea breezes are my constant,
dress me at their whim, disguise my intent. The jewellery I wear is free.
I walk these sands every Thursday and listen to the echoes
of my empty feet. The birds can hear it too, even the gulls avoid me.
The deafness of old age is misdiagnosed: what's happening is
your hearing is actually sharper, just not the things you want to hear.
But you don't have to believe me, not everything I say is true.

You don't want to hear the desperate bitterness of crabs or imagine
the beautiful bones of the boy you loved sprinkled across
a foreign shore or incarcerated in some fancy casket his family insisted
he have. Still, I listen out for him every Thursday, watching the waves.
I sealed his death with a kiss, he has to find me. Sometimes I come
to see the lighthouse flash, it reminds me of voyages I wish I'd taken
or those I didn't. In the end all we can do is walk and carry the sands
on our feet to leave at the doors of the lonely. But don't
listen to me, I was always being accused of too much fancy.

# There by the Waters of Margate
# I Sat Down and Wept

*For T. S. Eliot*

while the dolphins turned in the restless sea
and the fishermen warped their nets
and the troubled souls and the mournful seals
all turned their eyes to the skies
and my mind leapt like the troubled fish
in that tense and turbulent sea
where the birds like bulls ruled bullishly
and the mothers of sons not returned from the front
continued to shake their angry fists at the clouds
it was the beginning of the end and the end begins
on English shorelines where they dream of victory
at the ships pulling out for America's real and distant dreams
where pious men and upturned women bear their sorrow like queens
and the words i seek in my midnight keel
this language i'm bequeathed
are runners sent to the battlefield to gauge the critics
waiting there with their ink-filled pens and Vivienne's barbs
vultures, sirens, robbers, thieves waiting to pluck the eyes
of Tiresias not knowing he was already blind
not knowing my only defence is words and words
and always words that litter the landscape
indefinitely like the bleached bones of buffaloes
startlingly, consistently white on the prairies
of the New World.

# Mer Boy

Sometimes Mer Boy wishes he owned the night
with wings instead of fins
then he would be up there with the stars
instead of shedding his crystal skin to follow
the trail of lost and lonely boys chiselled
into the sand by hunger.
Breaking out of the sea by Newgate Gap, each time
he is reborn, with only the scant shimmer
of fine quartz on his nose and chin. Tonight
he's John Travolta strutting past the Clocktower
heading for the clubs with watery names like *The Ocean*
and *Atlantis*, time raising them from the deep
blood pumping round his be-jeaned thighs
hair skim-shined and bat-black
hunting the boys from Margate
dreaming of the moment he will draw them down
to Hades where he's lovingly building
a gallery of souls.

# 100 Olive Trees

They burnt the olive trees down
to the ground; aged trees that fed
and succoured generations, bowed their branches
to offer fruit, oil, shade. Their roots
ran deep in the earth – silent witnesses
to those who had toiled, tilled and planted;
spoke in tongues of comforting syllables, settled in the rocks,
travelled from place to place seeking a home.
*Their* stories are now atomised in the ash, crumbed
as millennial dust, broken as morning dreams, dispersed
as races. Who realises the bitter irony of proverbs –
*one does not bite the hand that feeds you –*
or the image of the olive branch as a symbol of peace?
No-one is listening now, not even
the wind whose only purpose it seems
is to offer a cooling breeze.

## and the thing is

if there had been a Brixton in the Home Counties
or a Cardiff in the Valleys
a Toxteth or a Chapeltown

where we could have dropped our Georgie bundles
where my mother could keep her church hat
and her accent
where she didn't have to always explain where she came from
where she could have kept her doilies and her Jesus
and slipped into familiar ways like others from the sun

if her laughter could have broken on backsteps
and carried upwards to the telephone wires
loud and raucous like parakeets
if carnival was not something to watch online
or remember from 1969
we could have cauterized some of the wounds
we acquired whilst migrating

south of the river in 1973 we couldn't get a plantain
you couldn't find an eddoe, saltfish or geera
sweet potato   bird pepper   callaloo
casyreep only come in somebody grip
travelling back from home

when the body have to force itself to dumb down
your forceripe self         and your chiffon dress
too flighty for the worship
when no hymns bursting     no tambourine
reverberating and the smiles are few over the pew

you are not easily identifiable    the colour of your skin
mystifies

because the thing is we didn't have no tribe
when you're half in half out   which half to throw out is the thing
which half can you reconcile as you watch tv the boys them get stop
over and over but nobody don't shove you
on the bus   or cross the road    or move house
that is the razorblade of misconception   the shame
you have to beat yourself to belong at the extent of denying
half of you    quarter of you   two cents of you
five shillings of you from Madeira to the Ivory Coast to Edinburrow

but her Jesus come with my mother who thank him for all he had done
bringing her and her children out of the wilderness
not understanding  was a different kind of wilderness

while letters from home full of murder and gangsta and riots
the Portuguese quarter where she born  now a no go
and even sugar you can't get even tho you grow up right there
nex the canefield our granddaddy breaking his back for forty years
we have to be thankful we have to be thankful we have to be thank

so we swimming in a different world and i not saying it all bad
the people did not massacre us with hate no dog
shit by the front door      tho once i got call a white nigger
my mother get call 'love' found work amongst those
whose hands were the colour of work
still they say we never knew people like you grew there

two generations later
across a pebbled beach in Kent broken
families are walking out of the sea
in wet shoes
their children and their mobile phones held high
above their heads
surrendering     their bodies to the Dover Patrol
i
n their wake    another broken trail
a human chain
from places formerly known    as home.

# Wales: A Tercet
## Sea, Earth, Time

## *Sea*

*La Mer, Mar, Mare, Mermother mother mother ...*
*Find me a rock to bare my breast. Find me a rock*
*to bare my breast. Find me a rock to bare my breast.*
*Marry me Sea, oh Husband Sea so a mermaid me i be.*
*The Sea, The Sea, the rolling Sea, Sea of Longing,*
*Sea of Stealth, Sea of Unbelonging.* Where seals roll
in the surf beneath black Pembrokeshire rocks
the Secret Beach whose name we shall not spill,
down through the cherry trees, down the path from
the Best Placed Garden Centre in The World,
following the myths of witches' cauldrons, climbing
the coast path to Dinas Head, paddle in the tideline,
from Aberporth where we run the dog. The froth
of waters is troubled with tales of the enslaved; black
and white and Nordic bones tussle in the deep.
The Irish Sea is never calm, the souls who perished
stir the waters endlessly: only the Romans stayed
their hand, consumed by Picts and Hadrian's Wall.
Seven times we crossed that sea, twice with the dog
who cried in the hold, three times I flew.

# Earth

*For days spent at 1 Green Meadow*

Every time we talked about selling
my heart cracked:
shattered glass the Snow Queen dispersed
around the earth, the splinters that lodged in the eye.
The hellebores spoke to me then, and the ferns.
The montbretia held their thousand breaths
and the poppies did what they did best:
opened their hearts and sang.
The stream ushered in a chorus, bardic
to the bone, altering its rhythm over the stones:
*you can't leave yet, we're not yet done,*
*the salmon haven't yet come home.*

# Time

*For Sadie*

After she was put to sleep, we drove to Abercych
and sat in the garden of The Nag's Head
by Afon Cych (a portal, they say, to the underworld).
We cried, remembering the joy
she had brought us, her golden body rippling
on beaches and woodland, or curled, happy
under a pub table. None of us came here to die.
We spoke of her first encounter with water, bounding
into Lake Windermere only to discover
the earth giving way. Instant swimmer, turning
full circle and paddling back to shore, her ears
like miniature oars. Or the time she took the wheel
of the campervan, preparing to reverse
into the Lampeter main road as we stood
on the drive nattering. Time held us still.
She was gone. And for years there would be
a dog-shaped hole between us, a space by our side
where our hands came to rest.

# Rules of Engagement with a Chocolate Cosmos

When the seed catalogue arrives ignore it; place it to one side as you
would junk mail, treat it like pizza delivery leaflets or holiday brochures
in summer.

Place it on the recycle pile.

Forget you requested it back in July when everything in the garden was
hanging baskets and lovely naked knees brushing past the brazen heads of
*Apollo Carmine*.

Place it on the just-in-case pile     just in case
you miss out on the chocolate cosmos you were too late in ordering last
year although the carmine of which you still have seed, is just as vibrant,
just as heart-stopping, as glorious as they salsa in the vicious winds that
sometimes descend into this garden
formerly known as backyard.

Do not on any account rip open that book of temptation. You know how
foolhardy such actions can be. Remember the price of compost during
lockdown. (Looking back, so much shit was free!). Your mistakes have
not been deleted. They emerge with your photographic memory as trays
of triffid seedlings taking over all surfaces in the kitchen, spreading like
fever throughout the house seeking every windowsill, shelf and dresser
anointed by the barest vagaries of light.

Remember, the key to good gardening is patience.
Patience and order. Think ahead. Select the right place, the right time.
Work with time itself as a corridor into a future that might never arrive,
tomorrows that remain as promises.

Leave it for a day or two
when you have that hour, that time for tea on the sofa when you can
contemplate your finances. Before you succumb, make the list you spoke
about when there was not one corner of your ten cent garden that was
not swathed by passion flowers and nasturtiums: that next year you would
not be so colour vulgar, next year will see the harmony, symmetry and
colour co-ordination that is the signature of real gardens designed to
promote the need of the human heart for ointment, salvation, restoration
and just enough wildness to face the world of rage, vacuum and loss.

And when at last your fingers
open those pages and your eyes have been mesmerised into a
kaleidoscope of shape and colour as limitless as the stars through tele-
scopes, be prepared for the urge to temptation: the lure like a fisherman's
hook dragging you into the eye of a zinnia
delightfully
described as *Reggae Orange*,
punching you into the dark galaxy of a *Black Magic* from the planet
of New Zealand
lurching you into the luminous spires of lupins
the ornate and sordid sunburst of *Helianthus Ms Mars*.

Be prepared for a fresh assault of gazanias, echinacea and coreopsis and
do not for one moment be swayed by the subtle seductions of bunny
mouths, popsicle petunias or steadfast geraniums patiently waiting to
re-inhabit this small earth in its flag-waving cosmic blast of hosannas.

# The Nightdream, Dante Gabriel Rossetti in a Birchington Graveyard

and when I went to find him I wandered the churchyard like a fool
skinning my eyes to read engravings grey as day and centuries smooth
on tombstones slipping drunkenly into the earth
*here lies here lies here lies*
propelled by beauty and lies I find him eventually right there
by the church door Christianity's last tussle to gain control
of the passage to the underworld and around him borders scramble
the roots of bramble and the rose where he sleeps in the arms
of the brotherhood.

# The Greenheart weaves a Tapestry of Songs

*To the tune of {partly} Billy Bragg, 'Hard Times of Old England'*
*'The hedgerows my grandfather tended have gone'*

On the road to Mahaica so the old story goes
A village called Perseverance I'm told
And there lives a tree full of much mystery
> *Oh the hard times of Guyana*
> *In Guyana were very hard times*

It stands on the highway, majestic and tall
Its trunk rising mighty while we are so small
And death waits for any who cause it to fall
> *Oh the hard times of Guyana*
> *In Guyana were many hard times*

They call it a Ceiba, a Silk Cotton Tree
The tree of the Dutchman, the Jumbie Tree
Haunted forever by the ghosts of slavery
> *Oh the hard times of Guyana*
> *In Guyana were many hard times*

Some call her Koomakka, some Halfway Tree
And come to appease her, child, woman and man
With prayers and offerings – cigarettes and rum
> *Oh the hard times of Guyana*
> *In Guyana were many hard times*

*Don't come near to the Jumbie Tree*
> *The Silk Cotton Tree the Koomakka tree*
*Don't come near with yuh chopper in yuh hand*
> *Don't come near with machete*
*Don't come near with cutlass*
> *If yuh scratch one scratch or thief one leaf*
*Is you will get chop not she*

*4000 miles away across the oceansea*
> *in a town called Plymouth, along Armada Way*
*Monsters creep in the middle of the night*
> *whilst the people sleep*

56

*Men with diggers, men with machines*

*m a s s s s s a c r e e e a a h h*

*One        Hundred        and        Ten        Trees*

*Their green hearts bleed through the cities, pour        into the waters of the world*

*Come to rest in the halfway tree. Bleed.*

# Notes

An excerpt from 'Only these grandmothers' was featured in Sharon Maas' novel, 'The Faraway Girl', 2021.

'A Pandemonium of Parrots' was published in *Locked Down Poems,* Poetry Space, 2021.

'Paper Patterns' was long-listed for Canterbury Festival Poet of the Year, 2020.

'There, by the Waters of Margate I sat down and wept' (for TS Eliot) was commissioned by Lucy Hannah and Speaking Volumes for BBC Arena 2021.

'Mer Boy' and 'The Migration of Ghosts' were published in *Seaside Gothic magazine.*

'100 Olive Trees' was published in *I am Not a Silent Poet*, Ed. Reuben Woolley, 2018

'and the thing is' won the Wales Poetry Award 2020 and was published in *Poetry Wales* and featured in Estuary Festival 2021.

# Acknowledgments

With deepest gratitude to all those who have encouraged me, from the UK, Guyana, and across the diaspora, with special mention to Jaime Pablo, 23/12/60 – 25/01/24, Guyanese football star, dub poet & digital creator whose online show *De Karna* showcased many Guyanese artists.

And with love and appreciation for my years in both Kent and Wales, for my family, warm friends and fellow poets from Thanet and Medway, from Canterbury to the Cellar Bards in Cardigan, and to Seren for believing in me and bringing these poems to life.

# The Author

Maggie Harris is Winner of the Guyana Prize for Literature, Regional Winner of The Commonwealth Short Story Prize 2014 and the Wales Poetry Award 2020. She has worked as Creative Writing tutor, Reader Development Worker and International Teaching Fellow and in collaboration with artists across genres since 1990. In 2024 she was awarded a DYCP (Developing your creative potential, Arts Council England) grant towards re-visiting Guyana and its rainforests, following the discovery of oil. She is published in journals including *Poetry Wales, Wasafiri, Magma, The Caribbean Writer* and *Seaside Gothic*. Her poem *Canterbury* is an Art installation in the city's Westgate Gardens, and her poem, 'Lit by Fire' on the North Foreland Lighthouse, was commissioned by the BBC. She has read her work internationally including the Caribbean, Ireland and India. Recent collaborations with artists in the US have put her poems to music: her poem, 'This is Not a Gospel Song' is on YouTube. In 2024 she was appointed a Fellow of the Royal Literary Fund and runs a weekly Reading Group in Kent. *I Sing to the Greenhearts* is her eleventh book.